Life Cycles

Milkweed Bugs

by Donna Schaffer

Consultant:
Richard Mankin, Ph.D.
USDA—Agricultural Research Service
Center for Medical, Agricultural,
and Veterinary Entomology

Bridgestone Books
an imprint of Capstone Press
Mankato, Minnesota

Bridgestone Books are published by Capstone Press
151 Good Counsel Drive, P.O. Box 669, Mankato, Minnesota 56002.
www.capstonepress.com

Library of Congress Cataloging-in-Publication Data
Schaffer, Donna.
    Milkweed bugs/by Donna Schaffer.
    p. cm.—(Life cycles)
    Includes bibliographical references (p. 23) and index.
    Summary: Describes the physical characteristics, habits and stages of development
of large milkweed bugs.
    ISBN 0-7368-0208-8 (hardcover)
    ISBN 0-7368-5699-4 (paperback)
    1. Large milkweed bug—Life cycles—Juvenile literature. [1. Large milkweed bug.]
I. Title. II. Series: Schaffer, Donna. Life cycles.
QL523.L9S36   1999
595.7'54—dc21   98-53032
                                                                                      CIP
                                                                                       AC

Editorial Credits

Christy Steele, editor; Steve Weil/Tandem Design, cover designer; Linda Clavel,
    illustrator; Kimberly Danger, photo researcher

Photo Credits

Bill Beatty, 8, 10, 12
David Liebman, 14–15, 16, 20
James P. Rowan, 6
Rob Curtis, 4, 18
Visuals Unlimited/Johnathan D. Spear, cover

1 2 3 4 5 6 04 03 02 01 00 99

Table of Contents

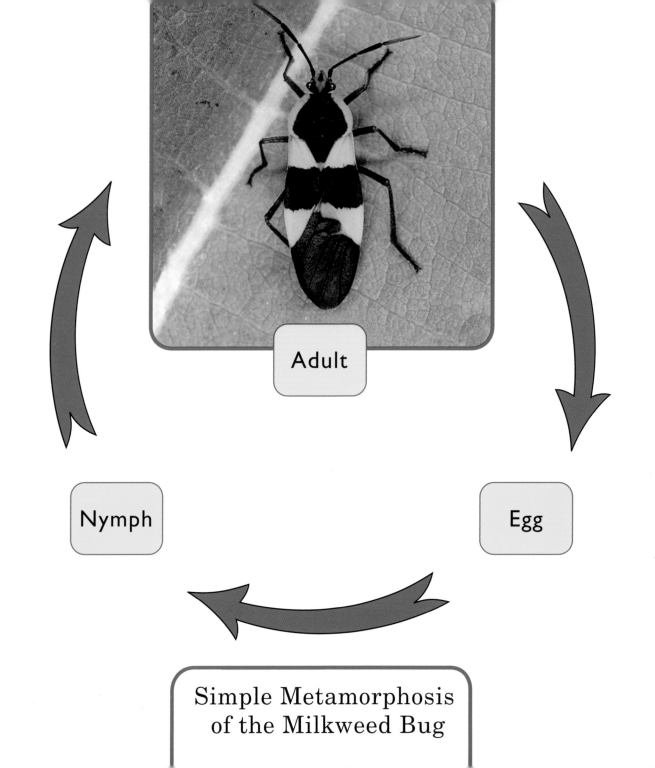

Adult

Nymph

Egg

Simple Metamorphosis
of the Milkweed Bug

The Milkweed Bug's Life Cycle

Milkweed bugs go through simple metamorphosis. This life process has three stages. A milkweed bug's body changes form three times during simple metamorphosis.

Milkweed bugs grow in eggs during the first stage of simple metamorphosis. Newly hatched milkweed bugs look much like adults.

Milkweed bugs are in the nymph stage after they hatch. Nymphs lack some adult body parts. Nymphs grow larger and develop adult body parts during this second stage.

Milkweed bugs are adults in the third life stage. Adults are fully grown. All of their body parts have developed.

These stages make up the milkweed bug's life cycle. Almost all living things go through cycles of birth, growth, reproduction, and death.

A True Bug

Milkweed bugs are insects. Insects do not have bones. They have an exoskeleton on the outside of their bodies. This hard covering protects and supports insects' soft bodies.

Insects have six legs and three body sections. These sections are the head, the thorax, and the abdomen. Antennas, eyes, and mouthparts are on the head. Wings are attached to the thorax. The stomach is in the abdomen.

Milkweed bugs are true bugs. True bugs are a type of insect. More than 4,000 species of true bugs live in North America.

Scientists call true bugs Hemiptera. This word means half wing. One-half of each outer wing is thick and hard. The other half of each outer wing is soft. Milkweed bugs also have two soft inner wings. Milkweed bugs use their inner wings to fly. Outer wings protect the soft inner wings.

● ● ● ● **Adult milkweed bugs are oval-shaped. Adults are black with orange-red markings. An adult's wings have red, orange, or black bands.**

About Milkweed Bugs

People named milkweed bugs after the plants they eat. Milkweed plants grow wild in fields and meadows.

Milkweed bugs are found only where milkweed plants grow. Milkweed bugs live in southern Canada, the continental United States, and central Mexico. More milkweed bugs live in southern areas than in northern areas. Milkweed bugs often cannot survive cold northern winters.

There are two kinds of milkweed bugs. Small milkweed bugs are 3/8 to 1/2 inches (10 to 13 millimeters) long. Large milkweed bugs are 3/8 to 5/8 inches (10 to 16 millimeters) long.

Milkweed bugs eat only milkweed plants.

Mating

Adult milkweed bugs mate to produce young. Adult males attract adult females by making a sound called stridulation. To make this sound, the males rub their back wings over their abdomens.

After attracting a mate, the male climbs on a female's back. The two bugs join their abdomens. They move around until each bug faces away from the other one.

Temperature affects how long milkweed bugs mate. In warm weather, the male and female may stay together for only one-half hour. In cold weather, they may stay together for more than one day.

Milkweed bugs mate in late spring or early summer.

11

Eggs and Nymphs

The milkweed bug's life begins on a milkweed plant. An adult female lays a brood of eggs. A brood may have up to 15 eggs. A female may lay two broods of eggs each year during her lifetime.

The eggs are oval-shaped and bright red. Each egg has three curved points near the tip. These growths help the eggs stay attached to milkweed plants.

Eggs hatch in three to six days. Milkweed bugs then begin their second life stage. Young milkweed bugs are called nymphs. Nymphs are red with black antennas and black legs. Their oval shape is similar to the shape of adult milkweed bugs.

Nymphs feed on the milkweed plants' flowers, pods, and seeds. The inside of the milkweed plant is full of a milky white juice called latex. The latex is gooey and hard to eat. The milkweed bugs have special mouthparts to help them suck up latex.

● ● ● ● **Nymphs grow larger over time. Some nymphs in this photograph are larger than others.**

Molting

A nymph outgrows its exoskeleton as it eats. The nymph must shed this outer covering to grow larger. This process is called molting. Scientists call the time between each molt an instar.

Nymphs grow a little bigger after each molt. They develop wings and their coloring slowly changes until their bodies are mainly black.

Nymphs molt five times before they become adults. After about 40 days, nymphs complete the final molt. They are fully grown and have fully developed wings. Milkweed bugs then are in the adult life stage.

Milkweed bugs shed their exoskeletons when they molt.

15

Survival

Adult milkweed bugs have bright orange-red markings. Birds and other predators can easily spot the bugs on milkweed plants.

The coloring of milkweed bugs warns predators. When milkweed bugs eat milkweed plants, they also eat harmful chemicals contained in the plants. The milkweed bugs do not become sick. But some animals that eat milkweed bugs can become sick. Predators recognize the colors and stay away from milkweed bugs.

Some predators still try to eat milkweed bugs. Milkweed bugs fly slowly. They are easy to catch. Instead of flying away, many milkweed bugs fall to the ground and lie still. The milkweed bugs seem to be dead. Predators often will leave them alone.

● ● ● ● **Milkweed bugs drink latex from milkweed plants. Chemicals in the latex can harm some animals. But the chemicals do not hurt milkweed bugs.**

Seed Bugs

Milkweed bugs are part of the Lygacidae family. This type of bug eats plant seeds. Some members of the Lygacidae family use plant seeds to travel.

Milkweed plant seeds float through the air on thin strings of the plant's silk. Wind carries the floating seeds far away. Adult milkweed bugs may hang onto the seeds.

Both the seed and the bug land in a new place. Not all milkweed bugs survive the trip to a new location. But if the seed grows into a plant, the life cycle of the bug continues in a new place. The milkweed bug lays eggs on the plant. The eggs hatch into nymphs that feed on the new plant.

● ● ● ● **Adult milkweed bugs may hang on to a milkweed plant's seeds.**

The Final Life Stage

Adult milkweed bugs live for about one month. They change color as they grow older. Young adults have orange markings. The orange markings turn red.

Adults eat milkweed plants during warm weather. During cold weather, the bugs leave the plants. They live in warmer places such as under leaves or logs.

Some adult milkweed bugs fly south during fall and winter. They live longer in warm southern areas. Milkweed bugs that live in cold northern areas do not live through the winter. Some bugs migrate north during summer.

The number of milkweed bugs is decreasing. Wild milkweed plants once grew in much of North America. Today, people are constructing buildings on the land where milkweed plants once grew. Milkweed bugs have fewer plants on which to live.

● ● ● ● **Milkweed bugs leave milkweed plants during cold weather.**

Hands On: Travel Experiment

Some adult milkweed bugs hang onto floating seeds. You can do this experiment to see how the bugs travel to new places.

What You Need

Five helium-filled balloons   Five strings

Five notecards   One hole punch

What You Do

1. Tie a string to each balloon.
2. Write your address on each notecard. Write directions on the notecard for the person who finds it. Ask the person who finds the notecard to send it back to you. Ask the person to write about where they found the notecard.
3. Punch a hole in the corner of each notecard. Tie a notecard to each balloon string.
4. Release the balloons outside.

The balloons carry the notecards much like plant seeds carry milkweed bugs. The returned notecards will show you how far the balloons have traveled.

Words to Know

antennas (an-TEN-uhs)—two feelers on the heads of some insects

exoskeleton (eks-oh-SKEL-uh-tuhn)—a hard, bony covering on the outside of an insect

instar (IN-star)—a stage between molts in the life cycle of certain insects

life cycle (LIFE SYE-kuhl)—the series of changes a living thing goes through

metamorphosis (met-uh-MOR-fuh-siss)—the changes some animals go through as they develop from eggs to adults

molt (MOHLT)—to shed an outer covering so a new one can grow

nymph (NIMF)—a young form of an insect; nymphs change into adults by molting several times.

Read More

Hunt, Joni Phelps. *Insects.* Close-up. Parsippany, N.J.: Silver Burdett Press, 1995.

Miller, Sara Swan. *True Bugs: When Is a Bug Really a Bug?* Animals in Order. New York: Franklin Watts, 1998.

Useful Addresses

Department of Entomology
Royal Ontario Museum
Toronto, ON M5S 2C6
Canada

Young Entomologists' Society
6907 West Grand River Avenue
Lansing, MI 48906

Internet Sites

FactHound offers a safe, fun way to find Internet sites related to this book.
All of the sites on FactHound have been researched by our staff.

Here's how:
1. Visit *www.facthound.com*
2. Type in this special code **0736802088** for age-appropriate sites.
   Or enter a search word related to this book for a more general search.
3. Click on the **Fetch It** button.

FactHound will fetch the best sites for you!

Index